SUPERSTARS

of

PRO
FOOTBALL

RAY
LEWIS

Jeremy K. Dunn

Mason Crest Publishers

Mason Crest
370 Reed Road, Suite 302
Broomall, PA 19008
www.MasonCrest.com

Printed and bound in the United States of America

CPSIA Compliance Information: Batch #SPF2013. For further information, contact Mason Crest at 1-866-MCP-Book.

First Printing

1 3 5 7 9 8 6 4 2

Library of Congress Cataloging-in-Publication Data

Dunn, Jeremy K.
  Ray Lewis / Jeremy K. Dunn.
     p. cm. — (Superstars of pro football)
  Includes bibliographical references and index.
  ISBN 978-1-4222-2722-0 (hc)
  ISBN 978-1-4222-9095-8 (ebook)
  1. Lewis, Ray, 1975- —Juvenile literature. 2. Football players—United
States—Biography—Juvenile literature. 3. Baltimore Ravens (Football team)—
Juvenile literature. I. Title.
  GV939.L49D86 2013
  796.332092—dc23
  [B]   2012037520

Publisher's note:
All quotations in this book are taken from original sources, and contain the spelling and grammatical inconsistencies of the original texts.

◄◄ CROSS-CURRENTS ►►

In the ebb and flow of the currents of life we are each influenced by many people, places, and events that we directly experience or have learned about. Throughout the chapters of this book you will come across CROSS-CURRENTS reference bubbles. These bubbles direct you to a CROSS-CURRENTS section in the back of the book that contains fascinating and informative articles and related pictures. Go on. ►►

◄◄CONTENTS►►

SUPER BOWL
CHAMPION AND MVP

As he exited the tunnel and headed onto the playing field of Raymond James Stadium in Tampa, Florida, Ray Lewis grabbed a few blades of grass and confidently proclaimed, "That's a symbol. This is our turf." This was not just an act of arrogance. It was a pregame tradition intended to motivate his teammates.

Ray, a middle linebacker on the Baltimore Ravens, was the key member of one of the most dominating defensive lineups ever to play in the National Football League (NFL). Ray and the Ravens were in Florida to play in Super Bowl XXXV—the 2001 NFL championship game. The Ravens were the American Football Conference (AFC) champions. Their opponents, the New York Giants, were the National Football Conference (NFC)

Linebacker Ray Lewis celebrates Baltimore's Super Bowl XXXV 34-7 victory over the New York Giants, January 28, 2001. For his inspired play with the Ravens' defense, Ray was selected as the game's Most Valuable Player.

Baltimore's Jamie Sharper (number 55) intercepted a pass tipped by his teammate, Ray Lewis (number 52) early in the second quarter of Super Bowl XXXV. Ray made 11 tackles, assisted on six others, and blocked four passes during the game.

champions. The Giants were next in line to face the wrath of the determined Ray Lewis and his defensive teammates.

The Big Game

With just under ten minutes remaining in the first quarter, Giants **quarterback** Kerry Collins threw a pass intended for wide receiver Ike Hilliard. Ray and his teammate Chris McAlister, who played the cornerback position, knocked down the pass to stop the Giants' offense. At that moment, Ray's confidence skyrocketed. He had completed his first defensive play of the Super Bowl.

CROSS-CURRENTS

For more on the place where the Baltimore Ravens won their first Super Bowl, check out "Raymond James Stadium." Go to page 46. ▶▶

From then on, Ray became a ruthless menace to the Giants' offensive players. He stopped New York's star running back, Tiki Barber, twice in the first quarter after gains of only two yards. In the second quarter, he tackled Giants tight end Howard Cross two yards away from a **first down**. Ray's biggest play of the game, however, occurred with just over eleven minutes remaining in the first half. Ray tipped a pass intended for Giants wide receiver Amani Toomer into the hands of his Ravens teammate, linebacker Jamie Sharper, for an **interception**.

As the Ravens headed into the locker room at halftime with a 10-0 lead, Ray was confident that his team could win. Before the game, he felt that 10 points would be enough for the Ravens to win the Super Bowl. Ray reportedly told two of his offensive teammates, Shannon Sharpe and Jamal Lewis, that if the team could score 10 points, the defense would shut the Giants down.

Throughout the second half, Ray and the Ravens defense maintained their stranglehold on the Giants' offense. As the final seconds on the game clock ticked away, excitement built among Baltimore fans. When the game ended, the Ravens had beaten the Giants, 34-7. Ray and his teammates were Super Bowl champions.

Super Bowl MVP

The Ravens' defense did their part in the victory by allowing the Giants only 86 passing yards and 66 rushing yards. Ray Lewis, who was already the NFL's Defensive Player of the Year, made five tackles and defended against four passes. Although it was not his best game ever, his tough play and leadership earned him the Super Bowl XXXV Most Valuable Player (MVP) award. It was only the seventh time in 35 Super Bowls that a defensive player had earned the MVP award.

In spite the top honor, Ray credited his defensive teammates in the NFL.com postgame report:

CROSS-CURRENTS

If you want to learn about the history of Ray Lewis's team, read "The Baltimore Ravens Franchise." Go to page 47. ▶▶

❝It was incredible to see the way we came out and played as a team. Our defense has been doing this all year. And never, never got the credit. No one can ever take this away from us. We're the best ever.❞

Murder Case Trouble

The Super Bowl triumph and the MVP Award capped a difficult year for Ray. On January 31, 2000—about a year before the Ravens won the Super Bowl—Ray and two of his close friends, Joseph Sweeting and Reginald Oakley, were involved in a fight outside of a nightclub in Atlanta, Georgia. The fight resulted in the stabbing deaths of two other young men, Jacinth Baker and Richard Lollar.

During the next five months, Ray maintained his innocence. On Monday, June 5, 2000, he accepted a deal to plead guilty to a **misdemeanor** charge of **obstruction of justice**. Under this deal, Ray would not face murder charges. The Superior Court judge sentenced Ray to 12 months of **probation**. In addition, he had to testify against Sweeting and Oakley. Although he was not charged with murder and no one was convicted of murder in the trial, the court case was painful for Ray. During the year, critics took every opportunity to treat him like a criminal. In a *Sports Illustrated* article entitled "The Gospel According to Ray," he said:

❝I hear everything from 'Murderer' . . . I hear everything from 'You shouldn't be playing football.'❞

In the days leading up to the Super Bowl, interviewers focused on Ray's past court case instead of on the Ravens' accomplishments and the upcoming Super Bowl against the Giants. In spite of the difficult questions, Ray persevered through the pregame interviews, with the

Ray speaks to reporters before Super Bowl XXXV. In the week before the championship game, many interviewers focused on the Baltimore linebacker's legal troubles, instead of on Ray's performance on the field.

loyal support of Coach Brian Billick and his teammates. When the game ended, Ray finally seemed at peace.

Even after the Super Bowl triumph, however, Ray continued to feel the effects of being connected to a murder case. Neither Walt Disney World Resort nor Wheaties cereal chose Ray to **endorse** their products. Traditionally, a Disney advertisement features the Super Bowl MVP boasting to the camera, "I'm going to Disney World," as he celebrates the Super Bowl victory. Ray did not share in that tradition. In addition, when General Mills made a Wheaties cereal box showing members of the Ravens celebrating their Super Bowl win, the picture did not include Ray.

FROM POVERTY TO THE NFL

Ray Lewis was born on May 15, 1975, in Bartow, Florida. He was the oldest of five children in a single-parent home. Ray's mother, Sunseria, worked two or three different jobs at a time. His younger siblings—twin sisters LaQuesha and LaKeisha, sister Kadaja, and brother Keon—needed a caretaker. Ray learned the meaning of responsibility at a young age.

When he was nine years old, Ray began handling chores and duties that are normally an adult's responsibilities. He became the "man of the house." Through caring for his younger siblings, Ray developed leadership qualities at a very early age. In an article in *Channel Magazine*, his mother recalls:

"By me working two to three jobs at the time, Ray became the man of the house. He cooked food, braided hair, and got his sisters and brother ready for the next school day before I got home from work."

CHANNEL MAGAZINE

Apr / May 2007

A Tribute to Mothers
Kellye Lynn, Meohelle Shields & LaDawn Black

Face Time
Attorney Warren Brown

Stay at Home Mothers

Our Beloved #52
Ray Lewis
Mom, Sunseria "Buffy" Smith

Ray Lewis and his mother, Sunseria "Buffy" Jenkins Smith, appeared on the cover of *Channel* magazine's April/May 2007 issue. As a teenager, Ray helped his mother take care of his four younger brothers and sisters.

Early Childhood

Sunseria "Buffy" Jenkins was only 16 years old when she gave birth to Ray. However, Ray's father, Ray Jackson, was not around much for his son. By the time young Ray was six years old, he hardly saw his father. In interviews, Ray has described the pain of growing up without his father. Eventually, Ray began to identify himself as Ray Lewis. This was the name of a close male friend of his mother.

As a teenager, Ray was able to balance all of his responsibilities. Although it was difficult at times, Ray attended school, participated in football and wrestling practices, and worked out until it was time for him to go to bed. He did all of this in addition to taking care of his younger siblings.

Wrestling Record Breaker and Football Star

Ray entered Kathleen High School in the shadow of his father. Not only did they look like each other, but his father held several wrestling records. Jackson's former coach, Brian Bain, gave Ray a list of all of his father's records. In an interview, Ray recalled how his absent father's records motivated him:

> **"Every one of those [his father's] records? I shattered them, and every time, I shattered them with pain. It was like, Yeah! It's over! His name is out of there!"**

Ray even won the 1993 Class AAAA state wrestling championship—something his father never accomplished. During his junior year in high school, Ray's mother remarried and moved away. In spite of their close relationship, Ray moved in with his grandparents so he could remain at Kathleen High School.

A star high-school football player, Ray was the team MVP in his junior and senior seasons. During his high-school career, Ray recorded 207 tackles, 10 **sacks**, and eight interceptions. As a running back, Ray gained 591 rushing yards and scored eight **touchdowns**. In addition, he scored four touchdowns as a punt returner and two touchdowns as a kickoff returner.

Freshman Sensation

Ray's high-school football success earned him a **scholarship** to play

When Ray Lewis was growing up, he had little contact with his father. As an adult, Ray has tried to be a good father to his own children. Ray also supports many programs that help children in need.

football for the University of Miami Hurricanes. Miami has one of the leading football programs in the National Collegiate Athletic Association (NCAA). As a freshman, Ray started the final five games of the season as a linebacker for the Hurricanes. In his first start, Ray made an impressive 17 tackles. He was named to the Freshman All-American Team after making 81 tackles, two sacks, and four pass deflections.

Although some critics thought he was small for a linebacker, Ray quickly emerged as one of the top defensive players in the nation. As a

CROSS-CURRENTS

Read "Miami Hurricanes" to learn more about the history of this school's highly successful football team. Go to page 48. ▶▶

Ray played three seasons for the University of Miami. In 1994, Ray's sophomore year, the Hurricanes finished 10-2 and played for the national championship. Overall, Miami won 27 games and lost eight while Ray was on the team.

sophomore, Ray proved that his freshman season was no fluke by leading the Big East Conference with 152 tackles. In 1994, he started every game at the middle linebacker position. He also made first team All-Big East Conference and first team All-American.

Trouble and Tragedy

While Ray enjoyed success on the football field, issues away from the game could have easily distracted him. He met a woman named Tatyana McCall during his sophomore season in 1994. Several months later, the two had an argument that resulted in Ray's first public run-in with the law.

According to a dorm resident assistant, Ray grabbed Tatyana, pushed her, and struck her in the face. Tatyana was pregnant with their first son, Ray III, at the time. Tatyana, however, never pressed charges against Ray and later claimed that she had started the quarrel. A year later, Ray attempted to break up an argument between Tatyana and another woman, Kimberly Arnold. Arnold claimed that Ray grabbed her and shook her. Once again, no charges were issued against Ray.

These problems never distracted Ray on the football field. As a junior, he made 160 tackles and was first team All-Big East and first team All-American for the second season in a row. Following his junior season, Ray decided to leave the Hurricanes and enter the NFL draft. He ended his college career with 393 tackles, six sacks, two interceptions, and one touchdown.

Just weeks before the NFL draft, Ray suffered a devastating loss. An intruder murdered his teammate and close friend, Marlin Barnes, and a girlfriend in the apartment that Ray and Barnes shared. Barnes was the teammate and friend who had always pushed Ray to do his best.

Barnes's burial was on the same day as the NFL draft. Ray always thought that the day an NFL team drafted him would be one of the most joyful days of his life. After losing Barnes, draft day was bittersweet. The Baltimore Ravens selected Ray Lewis in the first round of the 1996 NFL draft. He was the 26th overall draft pick.

CROSS-CURRENTS

To learn about the some of the great players drafted along with Ray Lewis, check out "The 1996 NFL Draft." Go to page 49. ▶▶

RISE TO NFL STARDOM

From the first time Ray put on a Baltimore Ravens jersey, it was clear he was an intense competitor. Before he put his heart and soul into football, however, he took care of his family. After signing his first contract with the Baltimore Ravens, Ray moved his mother, three sisters, and brother into a comfortable community in Baltimore.

Ray wanted to keep his family close together. Also, he wanted to move them out of a poor neighborhood and into a place where they would feel safe. Ray's mother, Buffy, was proud of her son. She would have been proud of him even if he did not play

Ray Lewis returns an interception for 18 yards during a 1997 game. Ray was drafted into the NFL before the 1996 season, and soon emerged as a defensive star. In his second season, he led the league in tackles.

professional football. Like Ray, she was determined to find success. In an article in *Channel Magazine*, she recalled:

> **"Ray would tell us, 'I am going to play in the NFL, I am going to make it!' I made up in my mind, I was going to be successful in whatever I did, if my son played ball or not!"**

Ray's generosity did not stop with his mother and siblings. He gave his father, Ray Jackson, $5,000 as an attempt to reunite with the parent who had not been there for him. Unfortunately, father and son did not reconnect.

Rising Star

On September 1, 1996, Ray played his first regular-season game for the Ravens. From his first game, it was clear that Ray was a leader. His first game was also the first game for the Baltimore Ravens franchise. The untested rookie made nine tackles and intercepted a pass in the end zone in the Ravens' 19-14 victory over the Oakland Raiders. After his first NFL game, Ray was picked as the AFC Defensive Player of the Week.

Although he was only 21 years old, Ray handled the pressures of professional football like a veteran. In his rookie season, he missed only two games, because of ankle and hip injuries. He completed his rookie season with two-and-a-half sacks, an interception, and 110 tackles. Ray's 110 tackles were the most of any Ravens player. With these numbers, Ray established himself as a feared defensive player early in his career. As a result of his early success, he was picked for *USA Today*'s NFL All-Rookie team.

In 1997, Ray proved that his solid rookie season had not been a fluke. In his second year, Ray led the NFL in tackles with 184 and was selected as a Pro Bowl player for the first time in his career.

In addition to accepting his responsibilities on the football field, Ray learned to accept responsibilities that are more important than football. In 1997, Ray and Tatyana McCall settled child-support arrangements in court. At

CROSS-CURRENTS

To learn more about the annual Pro Bowl, which showcases the NFL's best players, read "Pro Football All-Stars." Go to page 50. ▶▶

Cheerleaders perform before a Pro Bowl game at Aloha Stadium in Honolulu, Hawaii. After his breakout 1997 season, Ray was chosen to participate in the NFL's annual all-star game for the first time.

the time, Tatyana was pregnant with their second child together. Tatyana expressed her views on Ray as a person and father in a *Sports Illustrated* interview:

> **❝Ray has a huge heart and will help anybody in need if he's able. I would be remiss if I didn't say I was proud to be the mother of his kids. It's not always easy, but I am very proud.❞**

Despite missing two games in 1998 because of a dislocated elbow, Ray led the Ravens with 120 tackles. He also made two interceptions and three sacks. His impressive performance again earned him

Ray sacks Oakland quarterback Donald Hollas during a 1998 game, preventing the Raiders from scoring a touchdown. The Ravens won, 13-10. After Ray had another strong season in 1998, the Ravens rewarded their star linebacker with a big contract.

Pro Bowl honors. In November 1998, the Ravens rewarded Ray with a four-year contract worth $26 million, making him the highest-paid linebacker in the NFL. The following year, he led the NFL with 168 tackles—the second time in four years that he had led the league in tackles. For the third season in a row, he made the Pro Bowl.

CROSS-CURRENTS

Read "Defensive Positions" to get a better understanding of the requirements of Ray Lewis's linebacker position. Go to page 51". ▶▶

In spite of all of his personal achievements on the football field, one thing was missing. Ray and the Ravens had yet to qualify for the NFL play-offs. In 1999, the Ravens completed the season with eight wins and eight losses. It was the first time the team had ended a season without a losing record.

Magical Season

Heading into the 2000 season, the Baltimore Ravens were not thought of as Super Bowl favorites. Since 1996, they had won only 24 games versus 39 losses and a tie. During their first few seasons, however, the Ravens had pieced together an outstanding defensive team. Unfortunately for the Ravens, their undisputed leader, Ray Lewis, was in big trouble as the team headed into the 2000 season. Ray was involved in a double murder case that occurred in Atlanta during January 2000. Although Ray was not accused of murder—and although he testified against two of his friends, who were eventually acquitted of the murders—a number of people still blamed Ray for the tragedy, including the families of the victims. In addition, the NFL fined Ray $250,000 because he was involved in the case. League officials said he had performed "acts **detrimental** to the league."

Ray's coach, Brian Billick, and his teammates publicly supported him throughout the difficult season. With many people watching them, Ray and the Ravens played a remarkable season. They ended their season with a seven-game winning streak. Over the whole season, they won 12 games and lost only four. The Ravens' defense set an NFL record by allowing opponents to score only 165 points, the fewest ever in a 16-game season. Ray was selected as the NFL Defensive Player of the Year after making 138 tackles, three sacks, and two interceptions. On top of everything else, he made the Pro Bowl for the fourth season in a row.

The Ravens earned a spot in the playoffs as a **wild card** team. In the team's first playoff game, the Ravens defeated the Denver Broncos, 21-3. After beating the Broncos, the Ravens faced the AFC's top team, the Tennessee Titans. Although the Ravens were the underdog, Baltimore won, 24-10. Ray overwhelmed the Titans with 12 tackles. He also intercepted a pass during the fourth quarter and ran it back 50 yards for a touchdown to seal the Baltimore victory. One week later, in the AFC championship game, the Ravens easily beat the Oakland Raiders, 16-3. In that game, Ray recovered a fumble on the Oakland six-yard line during the fourth quarter. That turnover led to a Baltimore field goal.

After winning the AFC championship, Ray and the Ravens headed for the Super Bowl XXXV. Playing in Raymond James Stadium in Tampa, Florida, the Ravens crushed the New York Giants, 34-7, to win the biggest game of the year.

Over the course of the playoffs, the Ravens had dominated their opponents by a combined score of 95-23. Many NFL historians consider the 2000 Baltimore Ravens as one of the best defensive teams in history. After facing difficult questions regarding the murder case during the days leading up to the Super Bowl, Ray said in the NFL postgame report:

> **"To be where I was last year and to hear everyone say that it's going to affect me, I had a higher power that said everything's going to be all right. . . . And that's why I'm here right now. If you put this in a storybook, nobody would believe it."**

Tough Times

The Ravens followed up their Super Bowl season with another solid season. In 2001 Baltimore made it back to the playoffs as a wild-card team. After a 20-3 victory over the Miami Dolphins in the first round of the playoffs, the Ravens lost, 27-10, to the Pittsburgh Steelers in the second round. The loss to the Steelers ended the Ravens' streak of five consecutive playoff victories.

In the following season, the Ravens stumbled, ending the season with a 7-9 record. It was also the first season in which Ray faced a serious injury. In the fifth game of the 2002 season, against the

The Ravens celebrate as Ray holds the AFC Championship Trophy up in the air. Baltimore defeated the Oakland Raiders, 16-3, to advance to the Super Bowl. It was the first time that the franchise reached the NFL's championship game.

Cleveland Browns, Ray injured his shoulder. He missed the next five games. He retuned to the field for a game against the Miami Dolphins, but his shoulder kept bothering him. Ray spent the rest of the 2002 season on the **injured reserve** list.

A Man Of God

Many people consider Ray to be one of the NFL's most passionate players. Sometimes he may come across as cocky and arrogant. Many critics have accused him of showboating and trash talking, especially when he was in college. He will often point to his biceps after a tackle. During pregame warm-ups, he sometimes dances around the end zone to the music from the stadium speakers.

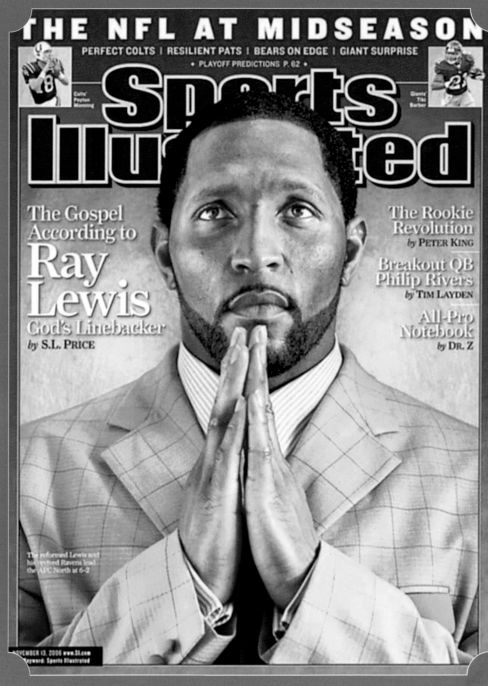

In a 2006 *Sports Illustrated* article, Ray Lewis spoke about his Christian faith. He has said that his troubles with the law in 2000 forced him to become a better person.

On the other hand, he devotes hours of his time during the week to carefully watching film of past games. He is the first player to help and advise his teammates, as well as congratulate them after a play. In an interview with the *Washington Post*, Kansas City Chiefs head coach Herman Edwards said in 2004:

> **"He's a full-speed guy from the time he comes out of the tunnel warming up till the end of the game. The way he plays, his passion for the game . . . . Does he talk about how good he is? Yeah, but he backs it up, too."**

Apart from his competitiveness and passion for football, Ray has another side to his personality. He has always had an appreciation for religion, but his interest in it increased after the murder trial in 2000. According to *Sports Illustrated*, he considers the murder trial as a blessing in disguise, because it made him realize that he needed a change in his life. As he walked out of the courthouse in June of 2000, he told his mother that he was a changed man.

Ray has followed the same path as Deion Sanders and the late Reggie White. Sanders and White are both former NFL players who used their fame in order to promote their faith in Christianity. Ray sees his success as caused by God and refers to God in many of his interviews. He says a prayer before each game. Also, prior to each game, Ray dips his fingers in **consecrated** oil and outlines a cross on the foreheads of some of his teammates and members of opposing teams. He fully believes that God has a purpose for him. In *Channel Magazine*, Ray said:

> **"God wanted to use me for a true testimony. Being great is not what you do, it is what you go through. There is nothing that will ever make me question God."**

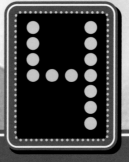

IN HIS PRIME

Ray could not wait for the start of the 2003 season. He was not used to sitting on the sidelines while his defensive teammates were out on the field. The shoulder injury that sidelined him in 2002 required surgery. Once he had recovered, he was out to prove that he was still one of the best linebackers in the NFL.

Ray had no doubt that he would be able to maintain his status as one of the best linebackers in the NFL. In an interview in *Football Digest* before the Ravens' 2003 season opener against the Pittsburgh Steelers, he said:

"I will just come out and play with energy. I want to see [Steelers coach] Bill Cowher's face when we play

In 2003, Ray showed that he was fully recovered from the shoulder injury that had sidelined him for much of the previous season. He made 163 tackles, forced a pair of fumbles, and picked off six passes.

Pittsburgh the first day. I trained harder than I ever did in the offseason. **"**

It was soon clear that Ray had not lost any of his ability or his intensity on the football field. His hard work during his off-season **rehabilitation** process paid off as Ray made 14 tackles and knocked down two passes in the game against Pittsburgh. The Ravens were thrilled to have the heart and soul of their defense back in the lineup.

Playing for a Childhood Hero

As a child, Ray idolized Chicago Bears linebacker Mike Singletary. The Hall of Fame player was everything Ray wanted to be as a football

During the 2003 season, Ray benefited from working with Mike Singletary, the Ravens' new coach of linebackers. Singletary had been a dominant linebacker during the 1980s and early 1990s, and was elected to the Hall of Fame in 1998.

player. When the Ravens hired Singletary as linebacker coach in 2003, Ray felt honored and thrilled. He told *Football Digest*:

> **"As a man, he will bring me everything I need in my life. As a coach, it will be special to know a guy I idolized and grew up watching is fighting for the same common goal. For my career, it will be a big bonus."**

Singletary had been a feared competitor on the field. He made his presence felt in each game he played. Among his greatest games was the 1985 Super Bowl, which the Bears won. Ray and Singletary had a great deal of respect for each other. Ray approached Singletary for advice on how to improve his football skills. More importantly, he was someone Ray could turn to when he needed a friend. Ray was not the only one who was impressed. Singletary was in awe of Ray from the first time he saw him on the playing field. In a *Sports Illustrated* article, Singletary said of Ray:

> **"[When I saw him play] I was seeing everything I missed. Only a few guys play the game with their hearts and their souls. A lot of guys don't know what you mean by that. You don't know until you hear it, and then you see it and you go, There it is."**

In their first season together, Ray had one of his best seasons in the NFL. He made 163 tackles and led all NFL linebackers with six interceptions. For the sixth time in his career, he earned a trip to the Pro Bowl. In addition, Ray won the NFL Defensive Player of the Year award for a second time. In winning this award twice, Ray joined an exclusive club. The only other players who had won the award more than once were Lawrence Taylor, Joe Greene, Bruce Smith, Reggie White, and Singletary.

CROSS-CURRENTS

Read "Brian Billick" to find out more about the life and career of the Ravens' successful head coach. Go to page 52. ▶▶

It was also a good season for the Ravens as a team. They qualified for the 2003 playoffs by winning 10 games and losing only six. Unfortunately, they lost 20-17 to the Tennessee Titans in the first round of the playoffs.

In 2004, Ray continued his outstanding play by recording 147 tackles, earning a place on the Pro Bowl team for the seventh time. The Ravens, however, missed the playoffs. Following the 2004 season, Singletary left the Ravens for another coaching job with the San Francisco 49ers.

Charity Work and Business

Ray's reputation on the football field is that of a rough, hard-hitting competitor who takes pleasure in tackling offensive players. Away from the football field, he is known as a generous person. He founded the Ray Lewis 52 Foundation—named after the number that he wears on his Ravens jersey—to make a difference and give back to the community. The Ray Lewis 52 Foundation is a **nonprofit** charitable organization that helps improve the lives of poor children.

Ray once adopted 10 families in the Baltimore area during the holidays and provided gifts for all of them. He also donated Thanksgiving meals and other necessities to 440 poor families in the Baltimore community. To promote education, the Ray Lewis 52 Foundation has teamed up with Office Depot and Frito Lay for an annual Back-To-School Kickoff event. Together, they provide 1,200 students with backpacks, school supplies, and snacks. Ray also regularly donates toys and Ravens tickets to families and children. His face lights up when he meets someone he has helped, especially if it is a child. In an interview in the *Baltimore City Paper*, Ray said:

> **"**Growing up—I wasn't the richest kid. So for me, to go back and give to a kid who has less material things— shoes, clothes, toys . . . during Thanksgiving I tried to feed over 400 or 500 families. And on Christmas I try to do Christmas drives. . . . It's what drives me to never quit in anything in life. Most kids don't realize it, they touch [my heart] when they tell me they love me and they watch me [play football on TV] all of the time.**"**

In 2004, he developed a friendship with Van Brooks, a young man who had suffered a severe spinal cord injury during a high school football game. Ray helped raise money for Brooks' recovery.

During a practice session before the 2004 Pro Bowl, Ray signs autographs for fans. Throughout his career, the star linebacker has often tried to meet younger fans and to help underprivileged children.

In 2006, Ray traveled with **Paralympic** gold medalist Cheri Blauwet to Ethiopia, where they developed a sports program for **landmine** victims. He also donated $67,500 for the development of a rehabilitation facility for **amputees**. Impressed by Ray's generosity, Blauwet had this to say:

❝Every time a child would pass within his field of vision, there would be a comment or an act that was very genuine, and he treated the people working with him that way. I got numerous lifts up stairs and onto airplanes. He would say, 'Hey, babe, let me give you a lift.'❞

In 2006, CBS broadcaster James Brown honored Ray with the Act of Kindness Award for his generous charitable contributions. Each summer, Ray hosts Ray's Summer Days, which is a charity event linked to his foundation. Ray's Summer Days includes a three-mile (five-kilometer) walk, a community festival, comedy, golfing, bowling, and other activities.

Aside from helping out in the community, Ray has also gone into business. In 2005, Ray opened up Ray's Full Moon Barbeque Restaurant, located in Baltimore's Canton community. He placed his two twin sisters, LaQuesha and LaKeisha, in charge of the popular restaurant. He also joined Hall of Fame running back Gale Sayers and businessman Mark Bloomquist to form S & L Racing. S & L Racing is a team that races cars and trucks in two of the National Association of Stock Car Auto Racing's (NASCAR) top series.

Fulfilling a Promise

Ray has always had a special relationship with his mother, Buffy. He always strived to make her proud. When her son graduated college, it ranked as one of Buffy's proudest moments as a mother. Ray left the University of Miami to join the NFL following his junior season in 1996, but he promised his mother that he would one day earn a degree. In May 2004, Ray graduated from the University of Maryland-University College with a degree in business administration. While he worked on his degree, Ray kept it a secret from his mother. He wanted his graduation to be a surprise, and it was. In an article in *Channel Magazine*, she said:

> **"I cried [because] that was such a surprise to me. It brought so much joy to my heart when he graduated."**

Fulfilling his promise to his mother to graduate college showed her how much Ray had matured over the years. In a *Washington Post* article, she said:

> **"What I'm most proud of with Ray is the man he has become, the man he is now, and the wisdom and knowledge that he has, putting God first in his life . . . . He has changed so much in his image, the right image he's supposed to have."**

Off the field, Ray Lewis has emerged as a successful businessman. In 2007, he was part of a real estate group that received permission to construct several new buildings in a poor section of Baltimore.

PlayStation®2

NTSC U/C

ALL-MADDEN

Riddell

RAVENS

52

EA SPORTS™

MADDEN
NFL 2005

EVERYONE

E

CONTENT RATED BY
ESRB

ONLINE™
BROADBAND AND DIAL-UP

Ray was featured on the cover of the video game *Madden NFL 2005*. The popular game by the software company EA Sports has sold nearly 6 million copies since its release in August 2004.

Madden Man

Following his Pro Bowl seasons of 2003 and 2004, no one doubted that Ray was one of the best, if not the best, defensive player in the NFL. In 2004, EA Sports, the company that makes the video game *Madden NFL*, chose Ray to appear on the cover of the 2005 version of the game. *Madden NFL* is the most popular football video game in the United States. Ray was pleased that EA Sports chose him as their cover athlete, especially after Disney World and Wheaties cereal had shunned him after Super Bowl XXXV, in spite of his MVP performance. In an interview with IGN.com, Ray said:

> **"**First of all, it's an honor to be on the cover because it shows the ultimate respect for what I do. And since in 2005 the game is definitely more defensive minded, not to mention the style and aggression of the game, that's me.**"**

Since he appeared on the cover of *Madden NFL 2005*, Ray has also endorsed Reebok, Under Armour Apparel, and Vitamin Water.

Ray hoped to follow up his *Madden NFL 2005* cover with another remarkable season, but a **hamstring** injury in the sixth game of the season sidelined him for the rest of 2005. The injury required surgery. In 2006, Ray was again healthy for most of the season, and he played in 14 of the 16 regular season games. By the end of the season, Ray led the Ravens with 103 tackles, made five sacks, and caught two interceptions. He earned his eighth Pro Bowl invitation, but did not attend the game because of a hand injury. His teammate Bart Scott replaced him. In 2006, the Ravens won the AFC North Division with a 13-3 record. Having the second best record in the AFC, the Ravens automatically made it to the second round of the playoffs.

CROSS-CURRENTS

To learn more about the popular video football game that Ray has endorsed, check out "Madden NFL." Go to page 52.

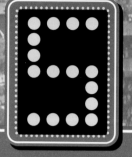

STILL GOING STRONG

Led by Ray Lewis, the Baltimore Ravens were the NFL's best defensive team in 2006. When the Ravens hosted the Indianapolis Colts in a divisional playoff game on January 13, 2007, fans in M&T Bank Stadium were confident that their team was destined to reach the Super Bowl again. The players felt the same way.

The Colts, led by quarterback Peyton Manning, were one of the NFL's most feared offensive teams. Some people felt, however, that the 2006 Ravens lineup was better than the Ravens lineup that had won Super Bowl XXXV in 2001. The Ravens appeared ready for the challenge. They did not allow a single touchdown by Manning and the Colts. Nevertheless, Colts kicker Adam Vinatieri kicked five field goals to score 15 points for his team.

The Ravens run onto their home field at Baltimore's M&T Bank Stadium. The Ravens' January 2007 playoff game against the Colts was a defensive struggle. Indianapolis emerged the winner by a score of 15 to 6.

The Ravens' offense let the rest of the team down, failing to score a touchdown and only scoring two field goals. The Colts defeated the Ravens, 15-6.

The playoff loss to the Colts was a bittersweet ending to a remarkable 2006 season. The Ravens believed that they could improve in 2007 and win the AFC championship. Ray was still the heart and soul of one of the NFL's most feared defensive lineups. Many football experts predicted that the Ravens would represent the AFC in Super Bowl XLII in February 2008.

Challenging the Undefeated

The 2007 season turned out to be a huge disappointment for the Baltimore Ravens. After 11 games, the defending AFC North

Ray tackles New England running back Laurence Maroney during a December 2007 Monday Night Football game. Ray made eight tackles and knocked down two passes, but the Patriots escaped with a 27-24 win to remain undefeated.

champions had only four wins. Their next opponent on the schedule was the New England Patriots. The Patriots had not lost a game all season, and their offense was among the most dominant in football history. Led by MVP quarterback Tom Brady and wide receiver Randy Moss, the Patriots looked as if they were on their way to an undefeated season.

Heading into the Monday Night Football game against the Patriots, several of the Ravens players—including Ray—were still mourning the recent death of a fellow football player. Washington Redskins safety Sean Taylor, a former University of Miami Hurricane, had been shot to death in his Miami home. As Ray told the *Baltimore Sun*, the death of Taylor had a great effect on him:

> **❝[T]he bottom line is I was more than a friend to Sean Taylor. I was someone he definitely looked up to. It's unfortunate that situations happen like this. But when they do happen, some things pull you away from everything else that everybody wants you to worry about.❞**

CROSS-CURRENTS

Read "Sean Taylor" to learn more about the young Washington Redskins defensive player who was tragically murdered in 2007. Go to page 54. ▶▶

Ray knew that he had a game to play, but his thoughts and prayers remained with Taylor's family.

Although the game was to be played on the Ravens' home field, few people thought Baltimore had a chance. The Patriots were favored to win by 19 points. The Ravens, however, came out strong and took a 10-3 lead at the beginning of the second quarter. The Ravens' defense continued to hound the Patriots' offense. By late in the fourth quarter, the Ravens still held the lead, 24-20. It looked as though Baltimore might be about to pull off a huge upset.

With less than two minutes remaining in the game, the Ravens sacked New England quarterback Brady on fourth down, one yard away from the first-down marker. That should have ended the game. However, Ravens defensive coordinator Rex Ryan had called a time-out just as the play was about to begin. Officials ruled that the play did not count, giving the Patriots another chance on offense. After this, the Ravens began to fall apart. In the last two minutes of the game, officials called five penalties against them, some of which were questionable. The Patriots took the lead for good when Brady threw a touchdown pass to wide receiver Jabar Gaffney with 44 seconds left in the game. The Ravens lost the game by a score of 27-24. Up to that point in the season, nobody had given the Patriots more of a challenge than the Ravens had. Ray made eight tackles in the disappointing loss.

If Baltimore had beaten the Patriots, the team might have turned its season around. Instead, the Ravens dropped to 4-8, then lost three of their final four games. The team that before the season had been expected to contend for the Super Bowl missed the playoffs altogether. It was a disappointing, frustrating season for everyone involved, especially Ray Lewis.

Father Figure

When he was growing up, Ray Lewis did not regularly have a father figure around. By watching his father slip in and out of his life, Ray learned what not to do as a father. He has tried to be a good father to his own six children—four boys and two girls. He spends as much time with them as possible. Ray has said that he wants to provide his children with the father figure he never had.

Although Ray does not live with any of his children full-time, he makes an effort to be a constant presence in their lives. Three of his children live near him in Baltimore, and three of them live in Florida. He tries to call each of his children daily. According to a magazine article, he schedules a movie date with his two daughters on Fridays. In addition, he sometimes allows all six of his children to stay at his home during the weekends the Ravens play in Baltimore. In an interview with the *Baltimore City Paper*, Ray was asked how he would live without football, if he had to. With much pride, he answered:

‟Oh, easily, [I have] my family, I have my three boys in Florida in track and football. Every time I see them come around the track, running with heart . . . see I don't worry about winning or losing. They know Daddy's over there. When I see my daughter in gymnastics and she runs over me to tell me, 'Daddy, look, I passed to a higher grade,' I shed a tear every time.”

On top of spending time with his children, Ray plans to open up a football training camp for high-school-aged boys in the summer of 2009. The camp will focus on improving defensive skills.

Still One Of The Best

Even though the 2007 season was a huge disappointment for the Baltimore Ravens, Ray proved that he was still one of the top defensive players in the NFL. At 32 years old, he was at the age when many football players—especially ones who play aggressive positions such as linebacker—begin to see their skills decline. That fact, along with the fact

CROSS-CURRENTS

For more information about the Ravens' place in the National Football League, read "AFC North Division." Go to page 55. ▶▶

Although Ray Lewis does not live with any of his six children, he has ___ to be more of a father figure than his own father was when Ray ___ growing up.

that Ray had suffered two season-ending injuries in the last four years, led some critics to believe that his career might be winding down.

Ray's solid 2007 season suggested that it was too soon to count him out. Although he missed two games because of an injury, Ray recorded 121 tackles, two sacks, and two interceptions. He was named to the Pro Bowl for the ninth time.

Still the Best in the League

Ray had another strong season in 2008. In the season's tenth week, he intercepted two passes against the Houston Texans, and also made eight tackles. Overall, Ray finished the season with 117 tackles, 3.5 sacks, three interceptions, two forced fumbles, and two fumble recoveries. He helped the Ravens return to the playoffs with an 11-5 record.

The team won its first two playoff games, defeating Miami, 27-9, and Tennessee, 13-10. This put Baltimore in the AFC championship game, where they would face the Pittsburgh Steelers. This time the Steelers were too strong, defeating the Ravens, 23-14, to advance to the Super Bowl.

After the season, Ray signed a new contract with the Ravens. The seven-year deal ensured that Ray would end his great career in Baltimore. In 2009 Ray proved the contract was a good deal for the Ravens. He led the AFC with 134 tackles and was named to the Pro Bowl for the 11th time. The Ravens made the playoffs again, and beat the Patriots in the wild card game. However, the next week Baltimore lost to Indianapolis to end their playoff run.

Playoff Disappointments

In 2010, the Ravens reached the playoffs again with a 12-4 record. Once again, Ray Lewis led the defense with 139 tackles. In the fourth game of the season, he picked off a pass from Steelers' quarterback Charlie Batch to seal a 17-14 victory. In Week 11, Ray picked off another pass, this time from Carolina quarterback Brian St. Pierre, and ran it back 24 yards for a touchdown. That was his 30th career interception, making him only the second player in NFL history to record at least 30 interceptions and 30 sacks during his career.

Ray chases a Cleveland receiver during a November 2007 game. That contest was one of Ray's best performances of the year. He made 16 tackles and ran an interception back 35 yards for a touchdown.

Ray Lewis remains one of the league's top defensive players. His coaches and teammates have said that they appreciate his leadership. Ray has been praised for working with younger players and helping them to succeed in the NFL.

In the wild card playoff game, the Ravens crushed Kansas City, 30-7. Ray forced a fumble that led to a Baltimore score. Their playoff hopes ended the next week, however, with a 31-24 loss to Pittsburgh.

The 2011 season was a challenge, as Ray missed four games due to injury. Despite this, he led the team with 95 tackles and was named to the Pro Bowl for the 13th time. The Ravens won the AFC North division with a 12-4 record, so they got a bye to the second round of the playoffs. There they beat the Texans, 20-13, to advance to the AFC championship game. There, the Ravens lost a heartbreaking game to the New England Patriots, 23-20.

What the Future Holds

At the start of the 2012 season, Ray was still among the top linebackers in the NFL. However, his season was cut short by injury. In the sixth game of 2012, Ray tore a muscle in his right arm. He missed the rest of the season.

Many people doubted that Ray would ever be the player he once was—or that he would even play again. Even though his contract runs through the 2015 season, he will be 40 years old. Few players—even all-time greats—have been able to compete in the NFL at that age.

As Ray approaches the end of his career, he already knows what is waiting for him when he retires. Aside from the Ray Lewis 52 Foundation and his business ventures, he plans to spend more time with his family. Whenever Ray decides to hang up his helmet and cleats, he will go down in history as one of the greatest linebackers ever to play in the NFL.

Raymond James Stadium

Construction on Raymond James Stadium, located in Tampa, Florida, and scene of the Ravens' 2001 Super Bowl triumph, began in 1996 and was completed in 1998. Tampa Sports Authority owns and runs the stadium. Raymond James Financial, a financial services firm located in St. Petersburg, Florida, owns the stadium naming rights. Raymond James Field is the home field of the NFL's Tampa Bay Buccaneers, as well as the University of South Florida Bulls. The stadium replaced the outdated Houlihan Stadium as the Buccaneers' home field. It opened its doors on September 20, 1998, when the Buccaneers hosted the Chicago Bears and won by a score of 27-15.

Raymond James Stadium is normally considered full with a crowd of 65,657. It can expand, however, to hold up to 75,000. For Super Bowl XXXV—which the Baltimore Ravens and the New York Giants played on January 28, 2001—Raymond James Stadium held an estimated crowd of 71,921. The stadium's seating includes at least 12,000 club seats and 195 luxury suites.

Raymond James Stadium is one of the NFL's top stadiums. Its field's turf is natural grass. In 2006, an NFL Players Association survey rated it as the best NFL playing field. Each year, Raymond James Stadium hosts the annual New Year's Day Outback Bowl. The stadium also hosted Super Bowl XLIII in February 2009. (Go back to page 7.) ◀◀

Raymond James Stadium in Tampa, Florida, was the site of the greatest moment in the history of the Baltimore Ravens franchise—the team's January 2001 victory in Super Bowl XXXV.

The Baltimore Ravens Franchise

Teams become part of the NFL when the league gives a team owner a franchise, or right to join the league. The Baltimore Ravens franchise played its first home game on September 1, 1996, against the Oakland Raiders. Football fans in Baltimore celebrated the Ravens' 19-14 victory.

Before 1996, the Baltimore Ravens franchise was called the Cleveland Browns and was located in Cleveland, Ohio. Founded in 1946 by Arthur McBride, the Cleveland Browns were one of professional football's most respected franchises. In 1995, owner Art Modell announced that he was moving his franchise to Baltimore. Modell wanted his team to play its home games in a new stadium, something the city of Cleveland could not give him. The Baltimore team took the name "Ravens" on February 9, 1996, separating itself from the tradition of the Browns. (Football in Baltimore was nothing new, however. From 1946 to 1984, the Colts had played in Baltimore until the franchise moved to Indianapolis, Indiana.)

Modell hired Ted Marchibroda to become the Ravens' first head coach. Jonathan Ogden, an offensive lineman, was the team's first draft pick in 1996. In their first season, the Ravens had a record of 4-12. In spite of the poor record, the Ravens sold out every home game in 1996. Fans in Baltimore were excited about their new team. Unfortunately, it took a while for onfield success to catch up to the fans' excitement. The Ravens failed to reach the playoffs in 1997, 1998, and 1999.

New coach Brian Billick replaced Marchibroda in 1999. After the 2000 season, the Ravens rewarded their fans with playoff success, including a victory in Super Bowl XXXV in January 2001. They also reached the playoffs after the 2001, 2003, and 2006 seasons. To date, the high point of the Ravens' history is the 2001 Super Bowl victory.

The Ravens' team colors are purple, black, white, and metallic gold. Their logo is a purple raven's head with a metallic gold letter *B* in the center. In 1998, the Ravens gave up their original logo due to an alleged copyright infringement. The original logo was a shield with wings and the letter *B* in the center.

Football in Cleveland was a precious tradition, as the Browns won four NFL Championships during the 1950s and 1960s. The relocation of the franchise to Baltimore devastated many of the Browns fans in Cleveland, who resented the relocation. Although the franchise's resources and personnel moved to Baltimore, the treasured identity of the Browns remained in Cleveland. In 1999, a new Cleveland Browns franchise began playing in the NFL. (Go back to page 8.) ◀◀

University of Miami Hurricanes

Ray Lewis played for the University of Miami Hurricanes from 1993 to 1995. The University of Miami has a rich history in college sports, especially football. The school's football program was established in 1926.

Fans debate as to where the name "Hurricanes" came from. Some say that the players held a meeting in 1927 to select a name for the team. They believe the team chose the name to imply that they were going to blow away the opposition, just as a ferocious storm blew through South Florida in September 1926. Others say the name "Hurricanes" was suggested because their first game was delayed by an actual hurricane.

From 1929 to 1941, the Hurricanes were in the Southern Athletic Intercollegiate Association. In 1935, the Hurricanes played in their first Orange Bowl—a college football game held in Miami every January—but lost 26-0 to Bucknell University. Eleven years later, the team defeated Holy Cross College, 13-6, to capture their first Orange Bowl victory.

As an independent team—that is, not part of a league or conference—the Hurricanes won the

When Ray Lewis was a member of the Hurricanes, the team played its home game at the Miami Orange Bowl. The university's logo can be seen in the center of the field in this aerial view of the stadium.

national championship in 1983, 1987, and 1989. In the 1980s, Miami won three more Orange Bowls, beating the University of Nebraska Cornhuskers, 31-30, in 1984; the University of Oklahoma Sooners, 20-14, in 1988; and the Cornhuskers, 23-3, in 1989. In 1990, Miami won the Sugar Bowl by defeating the University of Alabama Crimson Tide, 33-25.

In 1991, the Hurricanes joined the Big East Conference, one of the most prestigious and competitive conferences in the NCAA. High-profile schools such as Syracuse University, the University of Pittsburgh, Boston College, and the University of Connecticut were among the top teams in the Big East. In their first year in the Big East, the Hurricanes shared the national championship with the University of Washington Huskies. In 1992, Miami defeated the Cornhuskers, 22-0, in the Orange Bowl. In 2001, Miami won another national championship, when it defeated the Cornhuskers, 37-14, in the Rose Bowl. In 2004, the Hurricanes transferred from the Big East Conference to the Atlantic Coast Conference (ACC).

Andy Gustafson, head coach from 1948 to 1963, led the Hurricanes to 93 wins, which is the school record. Other noteworthy coaches in Hurricanes history include Jack Harding, Howard Schnellenberger, Jimmy Johnson, Dennis Erickson, and Larry Coker. The Hurricanes' colors are primarily green and orange, and their helmet is white with a green-and-orange letter *U* standing for "university." (Go back to page 13.) ◀◀

The 1996 NFL Draft

The 1996 NFL Draft, held on April 20 and 21, is known for the entry of some of the NFL's top wide receivers into the league. The New York Jets selected Keyshawn Johnson, from of the University of Southern California, as the first overall draft pick. Johnson was a key player on the Tampa Bay Buccaneers 2002 Super Bowl team. An even more accomplished wide receiver who entered the NFL in the 1996 draft is Terrell Owens. The San Francisco 49ers picked Owens 89th overall in the third round of the draft. Owens had previously played at the University of Tennessee-Chattanooga. Other noteworthy receivers who entered the league in this draft were Terry Glenn, Marvin Harrison, Amani Toomer, Mushin Muhammad, and Eric Moulds.

Ray Lewis is arguably the best linebacker who entered the NFL in the 1996 draft. Other star linebackers drafted into the NFL in 1996 include Kevin Hardy, Randall Godfrey, Tedy Bruschi, Donnie Edwards, and Zach Thomas. Running back Eddie George, fullback Mike Alstott, offensive guard Jonathan Ogden, and free safety Brian Dawkins also joined the NFL in the 1996 draft. (Go back to page 15.) ◀◀

Pro Football All-Stars

The Pro Bowl is the NFL's all-star game. Professional football has a long tradition of all-star events. The first pro football all-star event was held in Los Angeles in January 1939. The game featured a match-up between the 1938 NFL champions, the New York Giants, and star players from various other teams. The Giants won this first all-star showdown by a score of 13-10. The all-star game no longer existed following the 1942 season, but in January 1951, it returned with the name Pro Bowl. This version of all-star football featured the top players from the American Conference playing against the top players from the National Conference. Following the 1953 season, the game became a match-up of the NFL's Eastern Conference versus the Western Conference. From 1951 to 1972, the Pro Bowl was played in Los Angeles.

In the 1960s, there were two football leagues in the United States: the National Football League (NFL) and the American Football League (AFL). The NFL and AFL merged in 1970 under the banner of the National Football League—the NFL of today. The new NFL was made up of

A ceremony is held on the field at Aloha Stadium in Honolulu before the 2008 Pro Bowl gam *The NFL's annual all-star game is always held in Hawaii shortly after the Super Bowl.*

the American Football Conference (AFC) and National Football Conference (NFC). The league's all-star game, which featured a match-up between the AFC and the NFC, was called the AFC-NFC Pro Bowl.

In the Pro Bowl, the top players from the AFC compete against the top players from the NFC. Players earn a spot on a Pro Bowl team by votes from coaches, players, and fans. The coaches of the Pro Bowl teams are the coaches of the teams that lost the conference championship games. Former Pittsburgh Steelers coach Bill Cowher holds the record for the most Pro Bowl victories, with four. During the early years of the modern NFL, the Pro Bowl game was held in various cities, including Los Angeles, Seattle, Miami, and New Orleans. In 1980, the Pro Bowl was played at Aloha Stadium, in Honolulu, Hawaii, and it has been there ever since.

Since the merger, there have been 42 Pro Bowls. As of 2012, each conference has won 21 times. In February 2004, the NFC defeated the AFC by a staggering score of 55-52, in the highest-scoring Pro Bowl in history. The lowest scoring Pro Bowl occurred in February 1987, when the AFC defeated the NFC by a score of 10-6. Each year, a player receives the Most Valuable Player award. Former Oakland Raiders quarterback Rich Gannon is the only player to win the MVP award twice. (Go back to page 18.) ◀◀

Defensive Positions

Ray Lewis is a middle linebacker for the Baltimore Ravens. Linebackers are key members of a football team's defense. In addition to linebackers, other defensive players on a football team include the nose tackle, the defensive tackles, the defensive ends, the safety, and the cornerback. The nose tackle, defensive tackles, and defensive ends make up the defensive line. Generally, they go head-to-head with the opposing team's center, guards, and offensive tackles. Linebackers position themselves about three yards behind the line of scrimmage, which puts them behind the offensive line but in front of the cornerback and safety.

Linebackers have many responsibilities. One important task is to tackle the opposing team's running backs if they make it through the defensive line. Linebackers also defend against short passes, trying to knock them down or intercept them. If the linebacker can't stop a pass, he must tackle the receiver to keep him from gaining many yards. Sometimes, linebackers rush the opposing team's quarterback, hoping to tackle him behind the line of scrimmage.

Football coaches will position their linebackers in different parts of the field, depending on whether they think the opposing team plans to run or pass. The middle linebacker usually has a special leadership role. He is the player to whom the coaches tell plays. The middle linebacker then calls out instructions to his teammates as they line up. (Go back to page 21.) ◀◀

Brian Billick

The Baltimore Ravens hired Brian Billick as the team's head coach before the 1999 season. Before coming to Baltimore, Billick was the offensive coordinator for the Minnesota Vikings. In his first season as the Ravens' head coach, Billick led the team to eight wins. At the time, this was their best record ever. By one year later, in the 2000 season, Billick and his coaching staff developed an overpowering defensive team. After winning twelve games in the regular season, the Ravens breezed through the playoffs, eventually winning Super Bowl XXV in January 2001.

Billick and the Ravens missed the playoffs in three of the next five seasons. In 2006, Billick's Ravens set a new team record by winning thirteen games in the regular season but lost in the second round of playoffs. After a poor record in 2007, the Ravens management let Billick go. During his career as the Ravens' head coach, Billick led his team to 80 wins and 64 losses.

Billick and Ray enjoyed a solid relationship most of the time. They may not have agreed all of the time, but Billick supported Ray through his hard times in 2000 and 2001. (Go back to page 29.) ◀◀

Madden NFL

Madden NFL, which is produced by EA Sports, is the most popular NFL video game for systems such as the Playstation 3 and the Xbox 360. The game is named after and endorsed by John Madden, the legendary former Oakland Raiders head coach who is now a well-known television broadcaster and NFL analyst. The first version of the game, which was called *John Madden Football,* came out in the late 1980s. In 1990 and 1991, EA Sports released the game for the Sega Genesis and Super Nintendo video game systems. Since 1992, EA Sports has produced an annual updated version of the game.

During the 1990s the game's features and graphics were continually improved. It quickly emerged as the best selling NFL video game, because it offered the most realistic simulation of a football game. The game continued to advance in the 2000s as features such as online play were introduced. Online play allows gamers to connect to the Internet and play against other gamers in other locations.

Madden NFL's major competitor was ESPN's version of an NFL video game. In 2004, EA Sports made a deal that gave it exclusive rights to use NFL teams, players, and stadiums in the game. This deal prohibits any other company from creating and selling a video game that represents the NFL and its players, teams, and stadiums.

John Madden himself appeared on the cover of all versions of the game before 2000. Since then, NFL players have appeared on *Madden NFL*'s cover. They view it as an honor to be shown

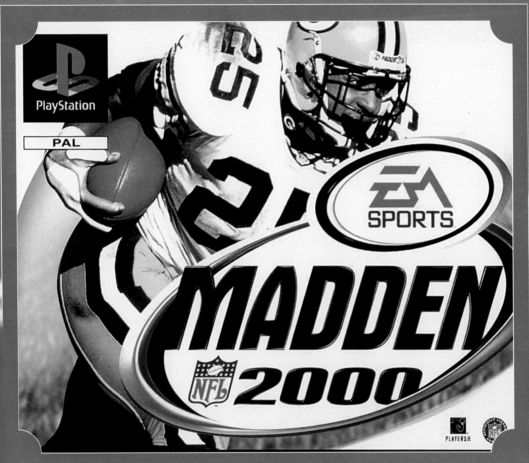

PlayStation

PAL

EA SPORTS

MADDEN NFL 2000

PLAYERS

The Madden NFL *video games are among the best-selling video games of all time. New versions of these realistic games, featuring NFL players, coaches, and teams, are released each year.*

on the cover of the popular video game. Some people, however, say that there is a "Madden curse." Many players who have made the *Madden NFL* cover have been injured after appearing on the cover. In 2002, quarterback Daunte Culpepper was the *Madden NFL* cover player, and he suffered multiple injuries the following year. The next two cover players, running back Marshall Faulk and quarterback Michael Vick, both suffered substantial injuries. After Ray Lewis was on the cover of *Madden NFL*, he suffered a season-ending injury in the sixth game of the 2005 season. Quarterback Donovan McNabb injured his chest in the first game of the 2006 season after he was the featured player for *Madden NFL*. In spite of the so-called cover curse, the video game's popularity has grown immensely over the past decade, and players still hope for the opportunity to appear on its cover. (Go back to page 35.) ◀◀

Sean Taylor

Washington Redskins safety Sean Taylor was murdered on November 26, 2007. That night, Taylor was in his Miami house with his girlfriend Jackie and their daughter, also named Jackie. Intruders broke into the house, and one of them shot Taylor in the leg. The gunshot severed his femoral artery, causing Taylor to bleed heavily. He was taken to a hospital, where he was pronounced dead the next morning. His daughter and girlfriend were uninjured.

Sean Taylor was only 24 years old at the time he was murdered. At the time he was killed, Taylor was a rising NFL star. If he had not been murdered, Taylor would have played his first Pro Bowl game in early 2008.

The week after Taylor's death, the NFL allowed all teams to wear a sticker with the number 21—the number on Taylor's jersey—on their helmets. The Redskins wore a patch with the number 21 on their jerseys. In remembrance of Taylor, there was also a moment of silence before the start of each NFL game. At the 2008 Pro Bowl, the three Washington Redskins who played—Chris Cooley, Chris Samuels, and Ethan Albright—all wore number 21 on their jerseys. The number 21 jerseys were auctioned off on NFL.com after the game. All the money from the auction went to Sean Taylor's Memorial Trust Fund. (Go back to page 39.) ◀◀

Sean Taylor (number 21, on the right in this photo from a Redskins' training camp) was a talented safety who was murdered in late 2007. Ray Lewis and others around the NFL mourned the 24-year-old's death.

AFC North Division

Each of the NFL's two conferences—the AFC and the NFC—is divided into four divisions. The fourdivisions of each conference are called the North, South, East, and West divisions.

Today, the Baltimore Ravens are in the AFC North division. Although the Ravens are a young team, they were not always in this division. Before 2002, the AFC and the NFC each had only three divisions—Eastern, Central, and Western. The NFL created the AFC North division (and the NFC North division) when they reorganized the two conferences in 2002. Before the 2002 season, the Ravens were in the AFC Central division with the Cincinnati Bengals, Cleveland Browns, Jacksonville Jaguars, Pittsburgh Steelers, and Tennessee Titans. The Ravens never won a division title while in the AFC Central Division. The Pittsburgh Steelers, on the other hand, won 16 AFC Central Division titles, more than any other team that played in that division. From 1972 to 1979, the Steelers won eight AFC Central titles in a row.

When the NFL added the Houston Texans in 2002, the league reorganized the conferences. The Ravens joined the Bengals, Browns, and Steelers in the AFC North Division, while the Jaguars, Texans, and Titans joined the AFC South Division. The AFC Central Division was eliminated, and other AFC teams were divided between the AFC East and AFC West divisions.

The Steelers won the first AFC North Division title in 2002 with a record of 10-5-1, while the Ravens finished third with a 7-9 record. In 2003, the Ravens won their first AFC North Division title with a record of 10-6. In 2004, the Steelers returned to the top of the division with a 15-1 record, while the Ravens finished second with a record of 9-7. In 2005, the Steelers and the Bengals tied for the division lead with records of 11-5. The Bengals won a tiebreaker and earned the AFC North Division title. The Steelers, however, went on to win the Super Bowl that season.

In 2006, the Ravens won their second AFC North division title with a record of 13-3. In 2007, the Steelers won their third AFC North Division title with a 10-6 record, while the Ravens finished last with a 5-11 record. This was the first time the Ravens had finished last in the AFC North.

The Ravens qualified for the playoffs as the wild card team in 2008 and 2009, finishing second in the AFC North both seasons. In 2010, they finished with the same 12-4 record as the Steelers. However, Pittsburgh had a better record in the division, so they were named the AFC North champions. In 2011 the same thing happened, but this time the Ravens had the better division record, so they won the AFC North title for the first time since 2006.

(Go back to page 41.) ◄◄

1982   Ray Lewis is born on May 15 in Bartow, Florida.

1989   Ray enters Kathleen High School.

1993   Ray ends his high school football career with 207 tackles, 10 sacks, eight interceptions, and 14 touchdowns. He wins the Florida Class AAAA wrestling championship.

In his freshman year of college, Ray starts five games as a linebacker for the University of Miami Hurricanes and is named to the Freshman All-American Team.

1995   After being named a first team All-American as a sophomore and junior, Ray announces that he will skip his senior year in college and enter the NFL Draft

1996   The Baltimore Ravens select Ray as the 26th overall pick in the first round of the NFL draft.

Ray is named to the USA Today NFL All-Rookie Team.

1997   Ray is selected to his first NFL Pro Bowl.

2000   On January 31, Ray and two friends are involved in a fight that results in the deaths of two young men.

On June 5, Ray pleads guilty to obstruction of justice and is given 12 months probation in return for testifying against the other men involved in the fight.

2001   On January 28, the Ravens defeat the New York Giants 34-7 in Super Bowl XXXV; Ray is the game's MVP.

2002   Ray misses eleven games because of a shoulder injury.

2004   On January 3, Ray makes 18 tackles in the Ravens' playoff loss to the Tennessee Titans.

2006   Ray leads the Ravens to a 13-3 record, the team's best season ever.

2008   Ray is selected for his ninth Pro Bowl in twelve years.

2010   Ray becomes the second player in NFL history to record 30 sacks and 30 interceptions in his career.

2011   The Ravens win their division and advance to the AFC championship game.

2012   Ray is named to the Pro Bowl for the 13th time; arm injury in the sixth game causes him to miss the rest of the season.

Career NFL Statistics

Year	Team	G	T	Scks	Int	TD
1996	Baltimore	14	110	2.5	1	0
1997	Baltimore	16	184	4.0	1	0
1998	Baltimore	14	120	3.0	2	0
1999	Baltimore	16	168	3.5	3	0
2000	Baltimore	16	138	3.0	2	0
2001	Baltimore	16	162	3.5	3	0
2002	Baltimore	5	58	0.0	2	0
2003	Baltimore	16	163	1.5	6	1
2004	Baltimore	15	147	1.0	0	0
2005	Baltimore	6	46	1.0	1	0
2006	Baltimore	14	103	5.0	2	0
2007	Baltimore	14	121	2.0	2	1
2008	Baltimore	16	117	3.5	3	0
2009	Baltimore	16	134	3.0	0	0
2010	Baltimore	16	139	2.0	2	1
2011	Baltimore	12	95	2.0	1	0
2012	Baltimore	6	57	1.0	0	0
Total		**199**	**2062**	**41.5**	**31**	**3**

Key:
G = Games played
T = Tackles
Scks = Sacks
Int = Interception
TD = Touchdowns

Selected Awards

Third-team All-America, 2004

NFL Defensive Player of the Year, 2000, 2003

AP First Team All-Pro, 1999, 2000, 2001, 2003, 2004, 2008, 2009

AP Second Team All-Pro, 1997, 1998, 2010

Pro Bowl selection, 1997, 1998, 1999, 2000, 2001, 2003, 2004, 2006, 2007, 2008, 2009, 2010, 2011

AFC Defensive Player of the Year, 2000, 2001, 2003

College All-American, 1994, 1995

NFL 2000s All-Decade Team

NFL Alumni Linebacker of the Year, 1999, 2003

Articles

Campbell, Rich. "Defending the Run 'Is Personal.'" *Washington Post* (December 8, 2006) p. E05.

Hanley, Lorna K. "A Mother's Love." *Channel Magazine* (April/May 2007): pp. 23-29.

Powell, Camille. "The Different Faces Of Ray Lewis." *Washington Post* (December 19, 2004): p. E01.

———. "For The Ravens, Season Continues to Be a Painful Process." *Washington Post* (September 30, 2007): p. D17.

Price, S.L. "The Gospel According to Ray Lewis." *Sports Illustrated*, vol. 105 no. 19 (November 13, 2006): p. 76-89.

Web Sites

http://raylewis52.com

Ray Lewis's official Web site includes a brief biography, career statistics, media updates, an online forum, an online store, and information about his Ray Lewis 52 Foundation.

http://baltimoreravens.com

The official Web site of the Baltimore Ravens includes the latest news about the Ravens team and players. It includes the team roster, photos, and video highlights, as well as the latest scores, schedules, and statistics. The Ravens' Web site includes an online forum for fans and an online store where fans can purchase Ravens merchandise.

http://www.nfl.com

The official Web site for the National Football League includes the latest news from all around the league, as well as the latest scores and schedules for all 32 teams. It also includes various player statistics and player profiles, as well as photos and video highlights.

http://www.nfl.com/superbowl

The official Web site for the Super Bowl focuses primarily on the most recent Super Bowl. It also includes a link to view the history of the Super Bowl, with statistics, scores, and records.

http://espn.go.com/

The official Web site for ESPN includes coverage for all professional and college sports. Visitors can read news articles, view full scoreboards, and watch video highlights.

amputee—a person who has had a limb, such as an arm or leg, removed from his or her body.

consecrate—to declare as sacred or holy.

detrimental—causing damage or harm.

endorse—to publicly express approval, as by appearing in an advertisement.

first down—in football, a possession of the ball by the offensive team that carries with it four chances to move ball toward the opposing team's goal; a gain of 10 yards gives an offensive team another four chances to advance down the field.

hamstring—either the two groups of leg tendons behind the human knee or any of the three muscles at the back of the thigh.

injured reserve—a record kept by a professional sports team's management indicating which athletes cannot play because of injuries.

interception—in football, a defensive play in which a member of the defensive team catches a pass meant for a receiver on the offensive team.

landmine—an explosive device designed to lie buried until it is triggered by someone walking over it.

misdemeanor—a wrongdoing that requires moderate punishment under the law.

nonprofit—not intended to make money for the owner.

obstruction of justice—a criminal charge in which a person interferes with a police investigation or a court trial.

Paralympic—having to do with a series of athletic contests for athletes with disabilities.

probation—the period of time in which a person must follow certain guidelines set by a court as punishment for a wrongdoing.

quarterback—the player on a football team who tells the team what play they are running and moves the ball to a running back or receiver after the snap.

rehabilitation—a process in which a person is restored to good health.

sack—in football, to tackle the quarterback behind the line of scrimmage, resulting in a loss of yardage.

scholarship—financial aid provided by a school or university for a student.

touchdown—in football, the carrying or catching of the ball beyond the opponent's goal line that is worth six points.

wild card—in the NFL, the teams with the next-best records to the divison champions that qualify for the playoffs.

page 8 "It was incredible to see . . . " NFL.com Wire Report, "Super Bowl XXXV MVP: Ray Lewis" (NFL.com, 2001), http://www.nfl.com/superbowl/history/mvp/sbxxxv

page 8 "I hear everything from . . . " S.L. Price, "The Gospel According to Ray Lewis." *Sports Illustrated*, vol. 105 no. 19 (November 13, 2006): pp. 76-89

page 11 "By me working two . . . " Lorna K. Hanley, "A Mother's Love." *Channel Magazine* (April/May 2007): pp. 23-29

page 12 "Every one of those . . . " Price, "The Gospel According to Ray Lewis," 76-89

page 18 "Ray would tell us . . . " Hanley, "A Mother's Love," 23

page 19 "Ray has a huge heart . . . " Price, "The Gospel According to Ray Lewis," 76-89

page 22 "To be where I was . . . " NFL.com Wire Report, "Super Bowl XXXV MVP: Ray Lewis," http://www.nfl.com/superbowl/history/mvp/sbxxxv

page 25 "He's a full-speed guy . . . " Camille Powell, "The Different Faces Of Ray Lewis." *Washington Post* (December 19, 2004): p. E01

page 25 "God wanted to use me . . . " Hanley, "A Mother's Love," 24

page 26 "I will just come out . . . " Tom Worgo, "A Man on a Mission," (Football Digest, October 1, 2003), http://findarticles.com/p/articles/mi_m0FCL/is_2_33/ai_107524511/pg_1

page 29 "As a man . . . " Tom Worgo, "A Man on a Mission," http://findarticles.com/p/articles/mi_m0FCL/is_2_33/ai_107524511/pg_1

page 29 "I was seeing everything . . . " Price, "The Gospel According to Ray Lewis," 76-89

page 30 "Growing up, I wasn't . . . " Christina Royster-Hemby, "Ray Lewis," (Baltimore: Baltimore City Paper, June 7, 2006), http://www.citypaper.com/news/story.asp?id=11905

page 31 "Every time a child . . . " Price, "The Gospel According to Ray Lewis," 76-89

page 32 "I cried (because) that . . . " Hanley, "A Mother's Love," 25

page 32 "What I'm most proud . . . " Powell, "The Different Faces Of Ray," E04

page 35 "First of all . . . " Jon Robinson, "Ray Lewis Interview—Madden Cover Athlete Puts the Hit In Stick," Sports.IGN.com, http://sports.ign.com/articles/521/521080p1.html

page 39 "[T]he bottom line is . . . " Jamison Hensley, "Ravens Central: Ravens' Ray Lewis On the Passing Of Sean Taylor" (Baltimore: Baltimore Sun, November 29, 2007), http://weblogs.baltimoresun.com/sports/ravens/blog/2007/11/

page 40 "Oh, easily, [I have] my family . . . " Royster-Hemby, "Ray Lewis," http://www.citypaper.com/news/story.asp?id=11905

Numbers in **bold italics** refer to captions.

Jeremy K. Dunn lives in Harlem, Georgia, with his wife Tonya and children Caitlyn, Chase, Landen, and Gavin. He is a Feature Writer for *Suite 101 Online Magazine* and has written for numerous online publications, including *Speedway Media*. He has earned a Certificate in Introduction to Internet Writing Markets from Georgia Southern.

PICTURE CREDITS

page

5: Woody Marshall/Macon Telegraph/KRT
6: The State/KRT
9: Orlando Sentinel/KRT
11: Channel Magazine/NMI
13: Elkman/CIC Photos
14: Mike Powell/Allsport/Getty Images
17: Harry Walker/KRT
19: Yukitake/T&T/IOA Photos
20: Steve Deslich/KRT
23: Larry Strong/Contra Costa Times/KRT
24: Sports Illustrated/NMI
27: George Bridges/KRT
28: Steve Deslich/KRT

31: Kirby Lee/NFL/WireImage
33: Channel Magazine/PRMS
34: EA Sports/NMI
37: T&T/IOA Photos
38: George Bridges/MCT
41: George Bridges/MCT
43: throwinrocks/AASI Photos
44: Keith Allison/SPCS
46: Marc Averette/T&T/IOA Photos
48: Miami Herald/KRT
50: Zack Everson/SPCS
53: EA Sports/NMI
54: D.B. King/SPCS